OCEAN ANIMALS

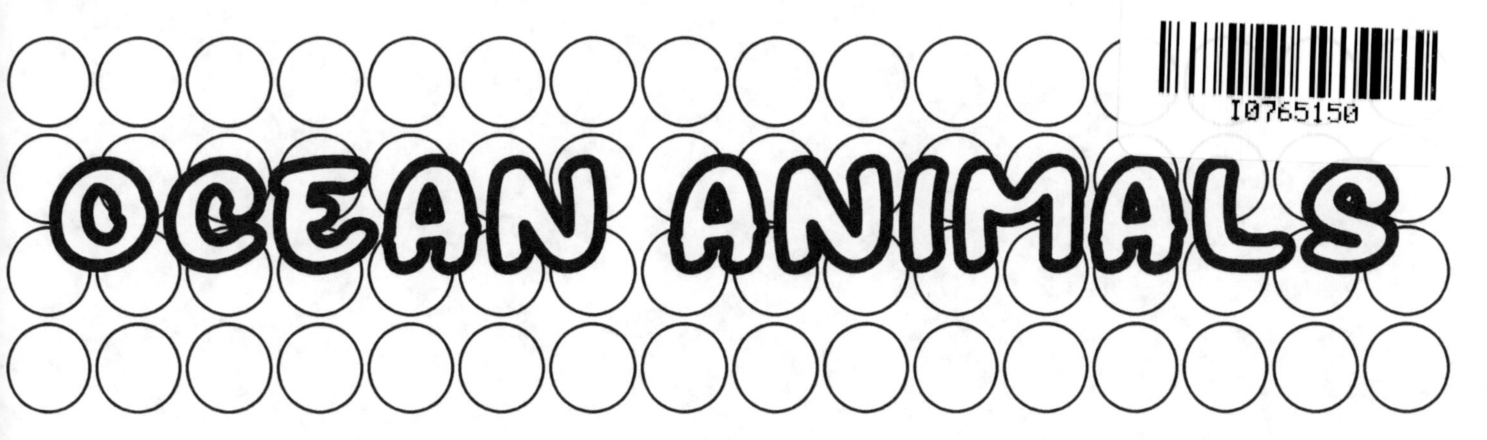

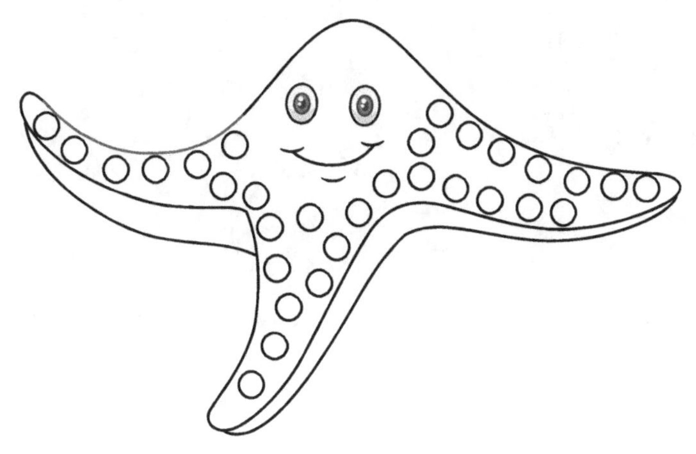

DOT MARKERS ACTIVITY BOOK

This Books Belongs To

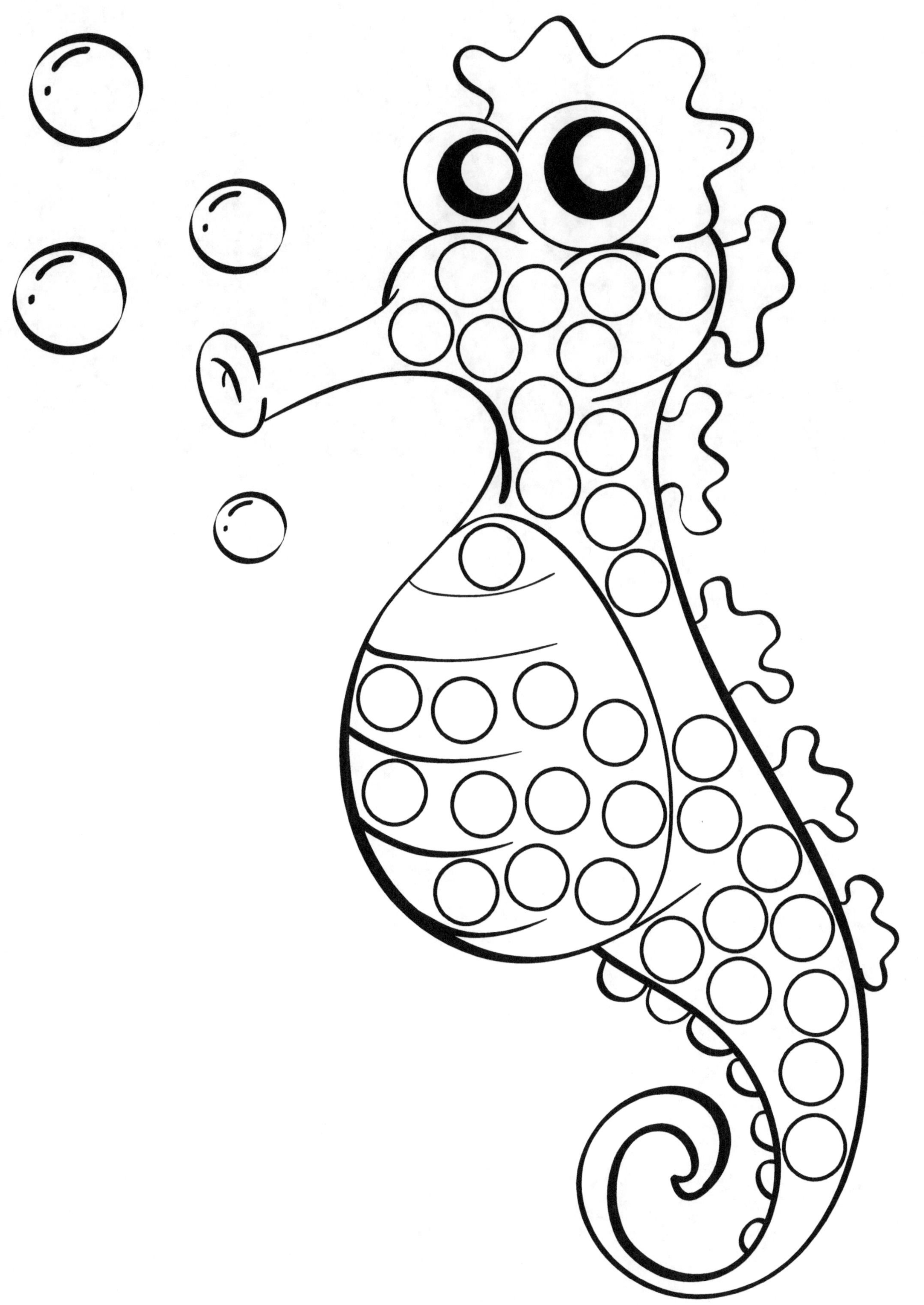

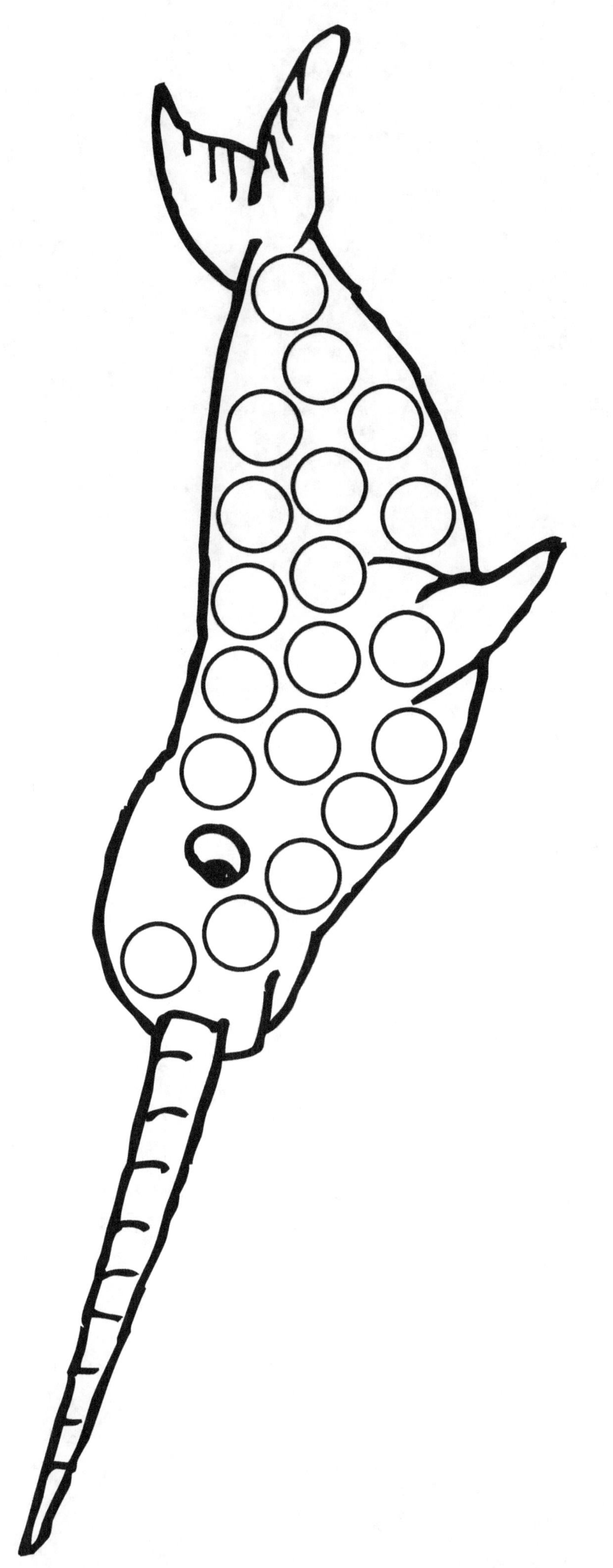

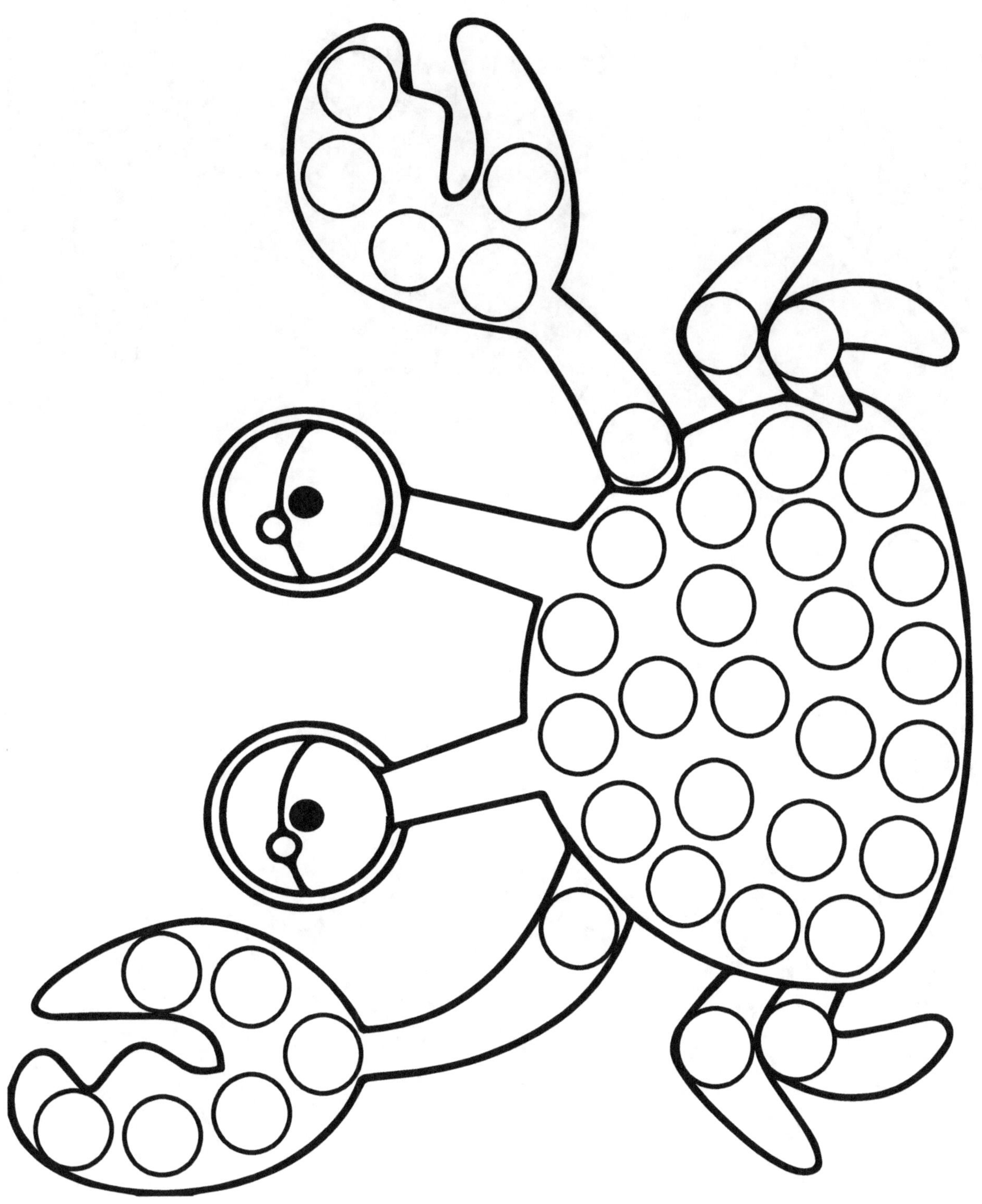

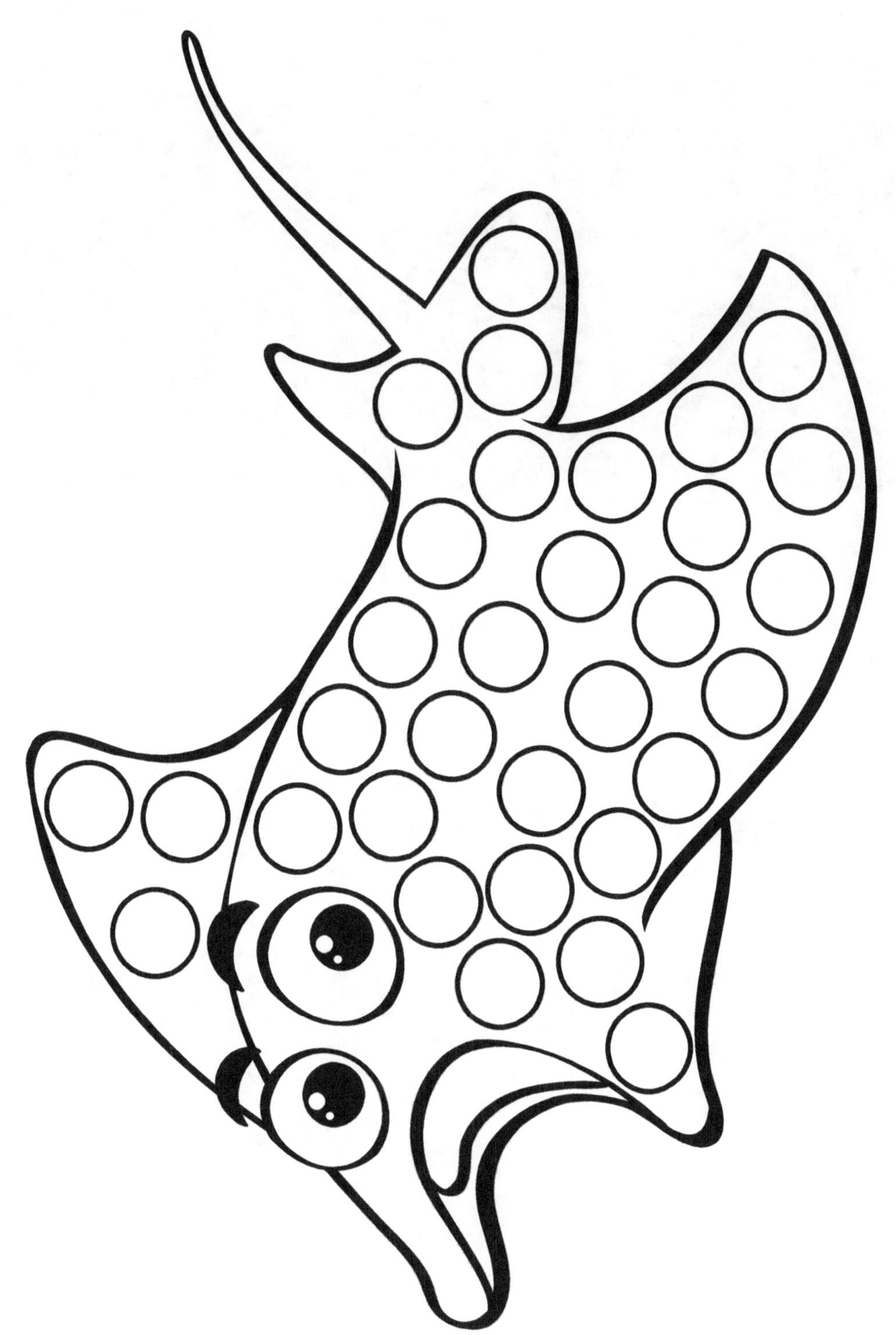

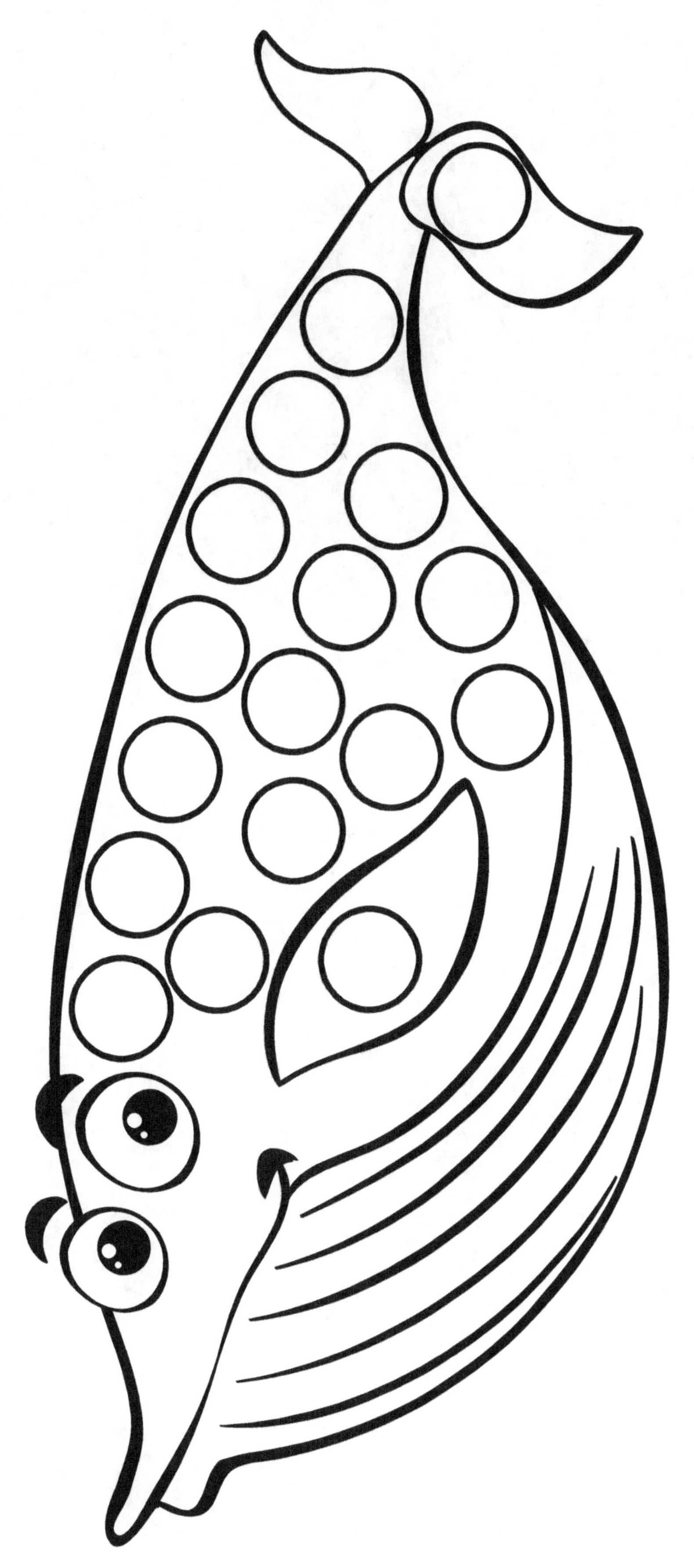

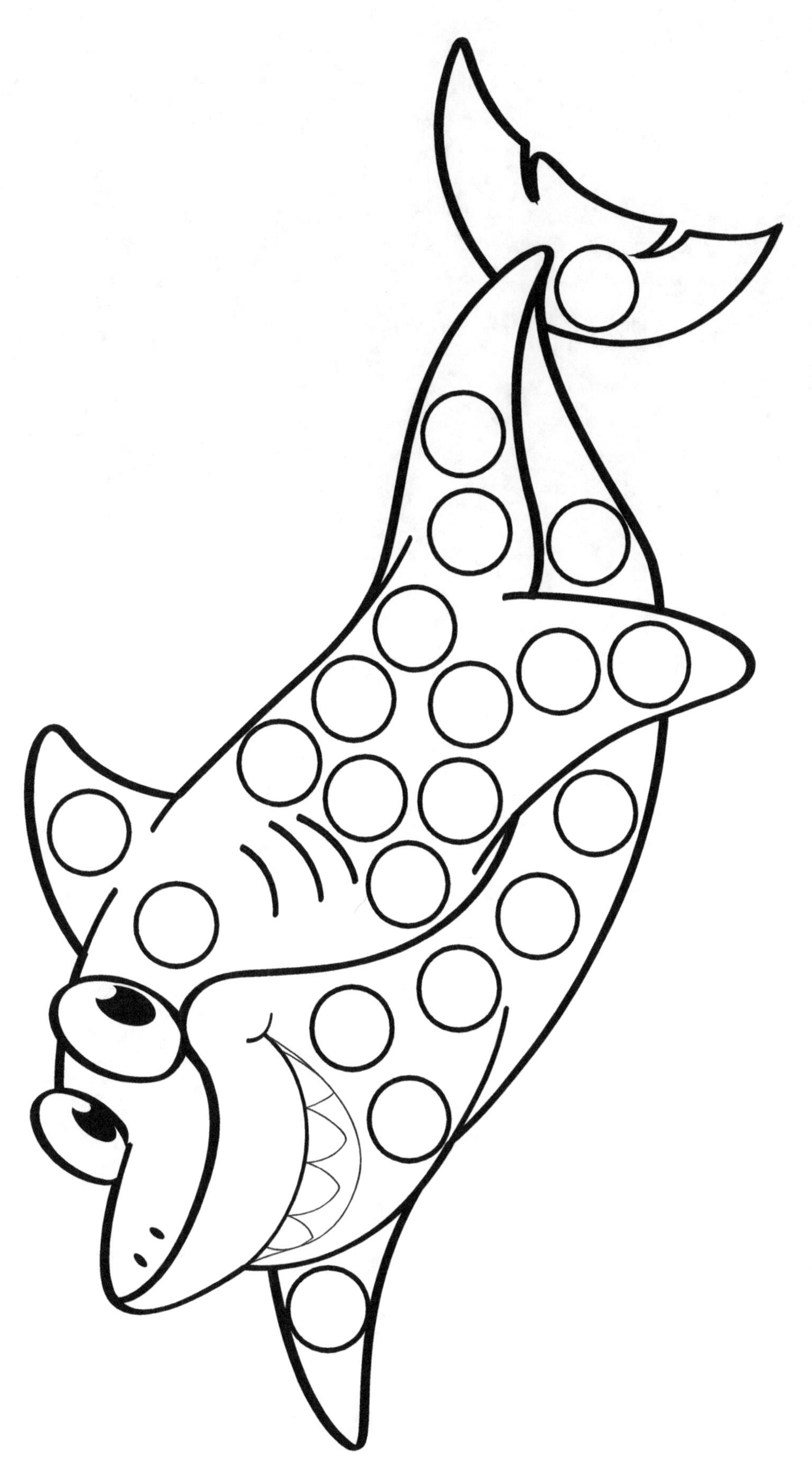

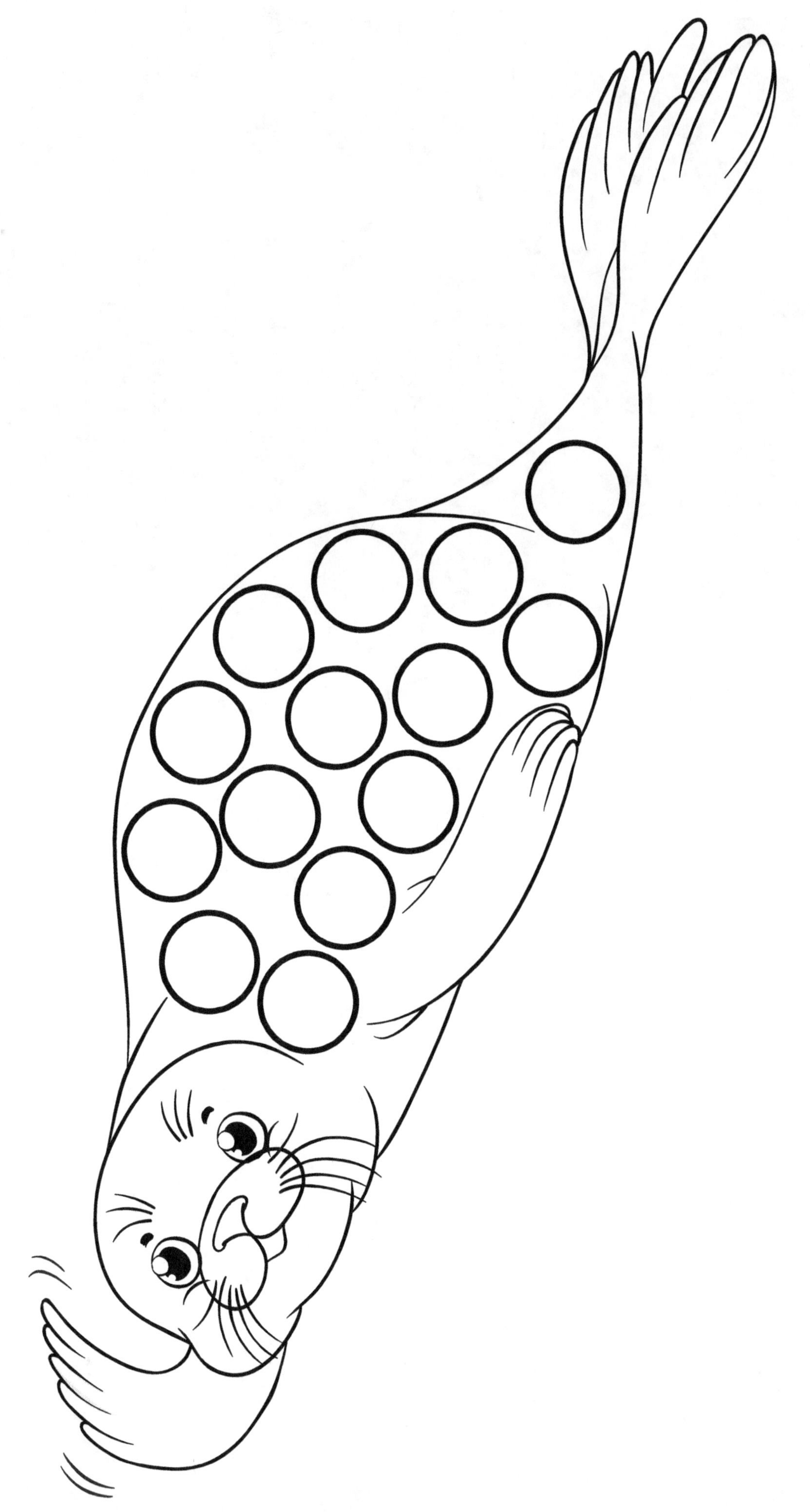

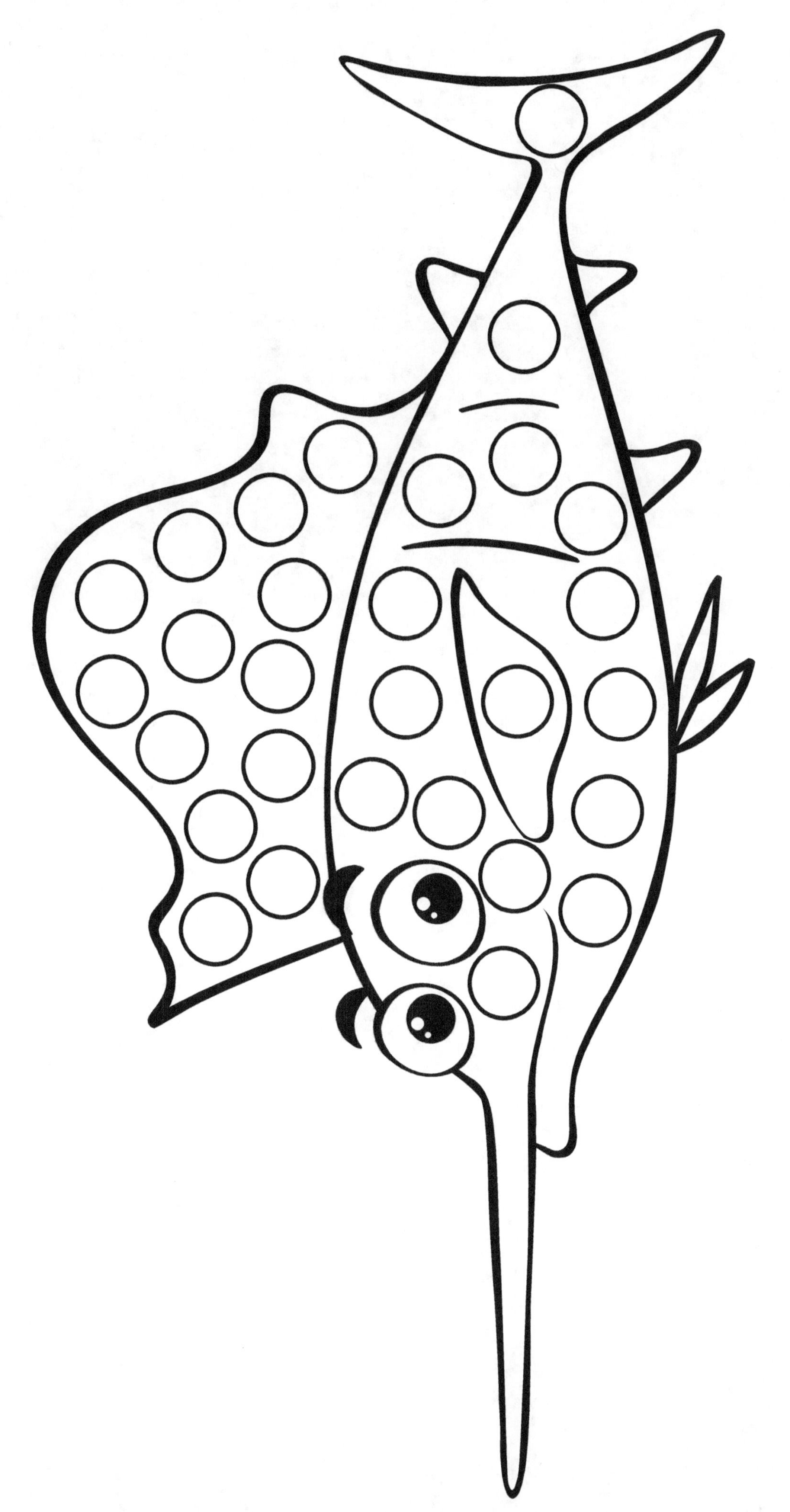

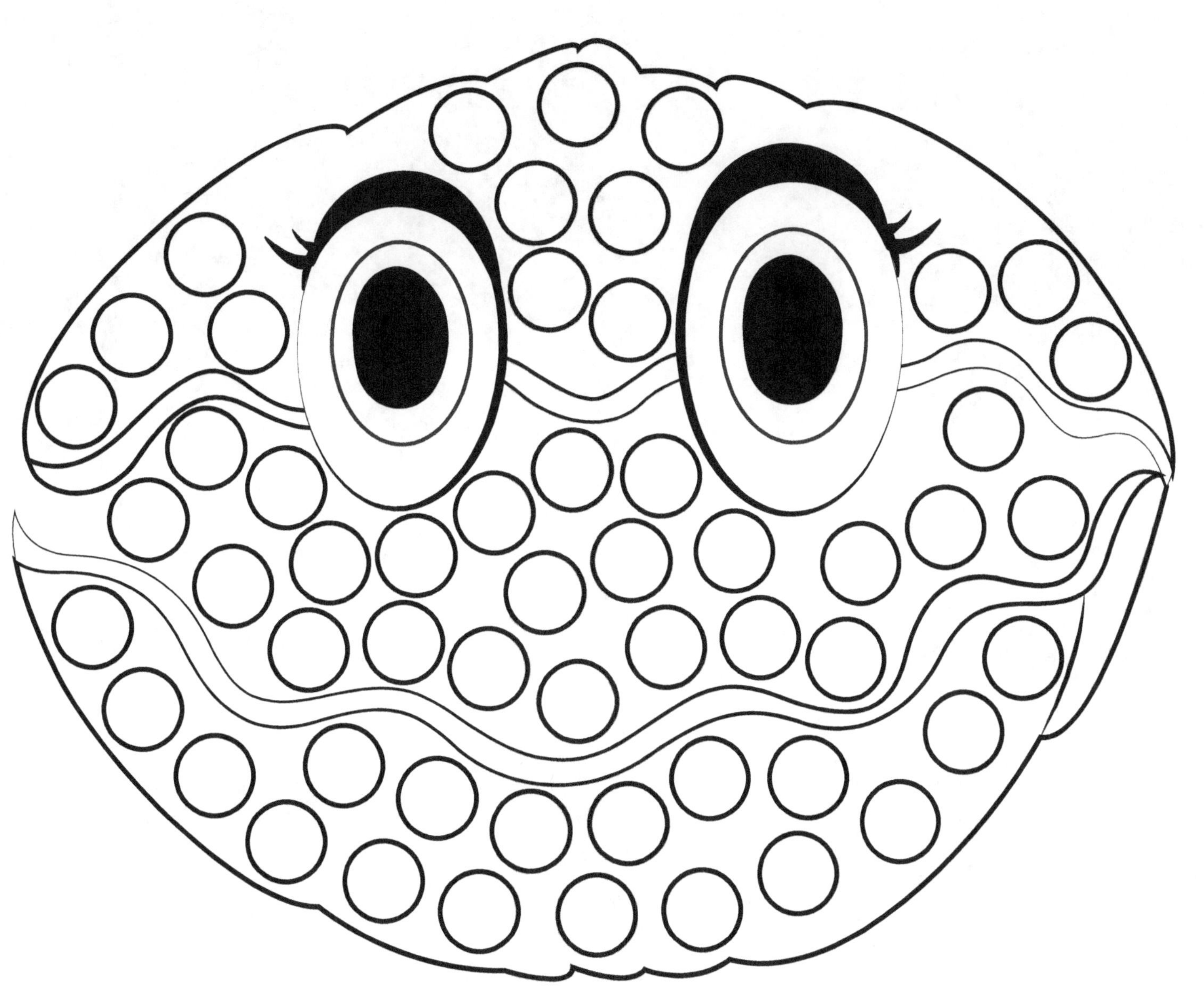

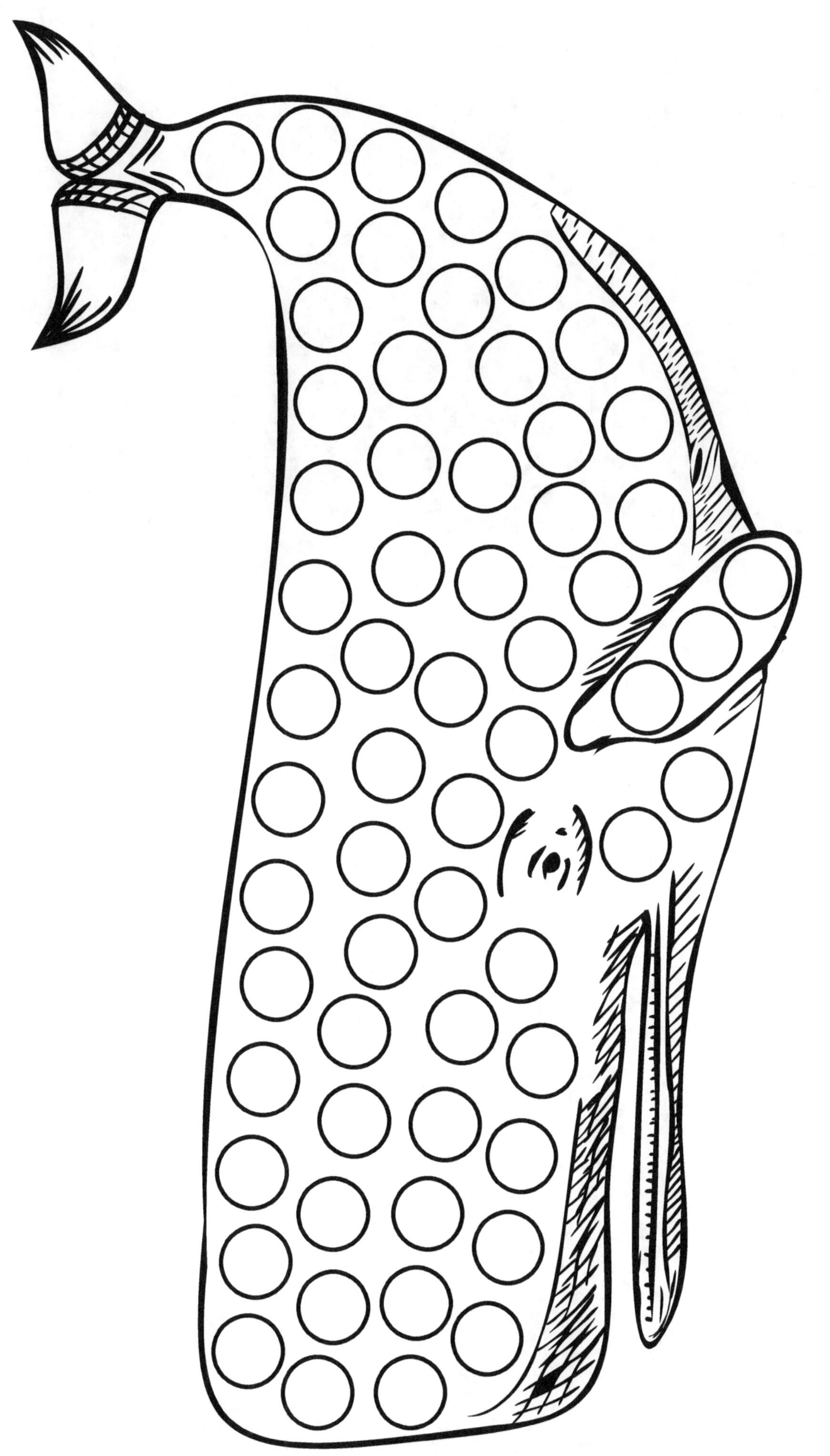

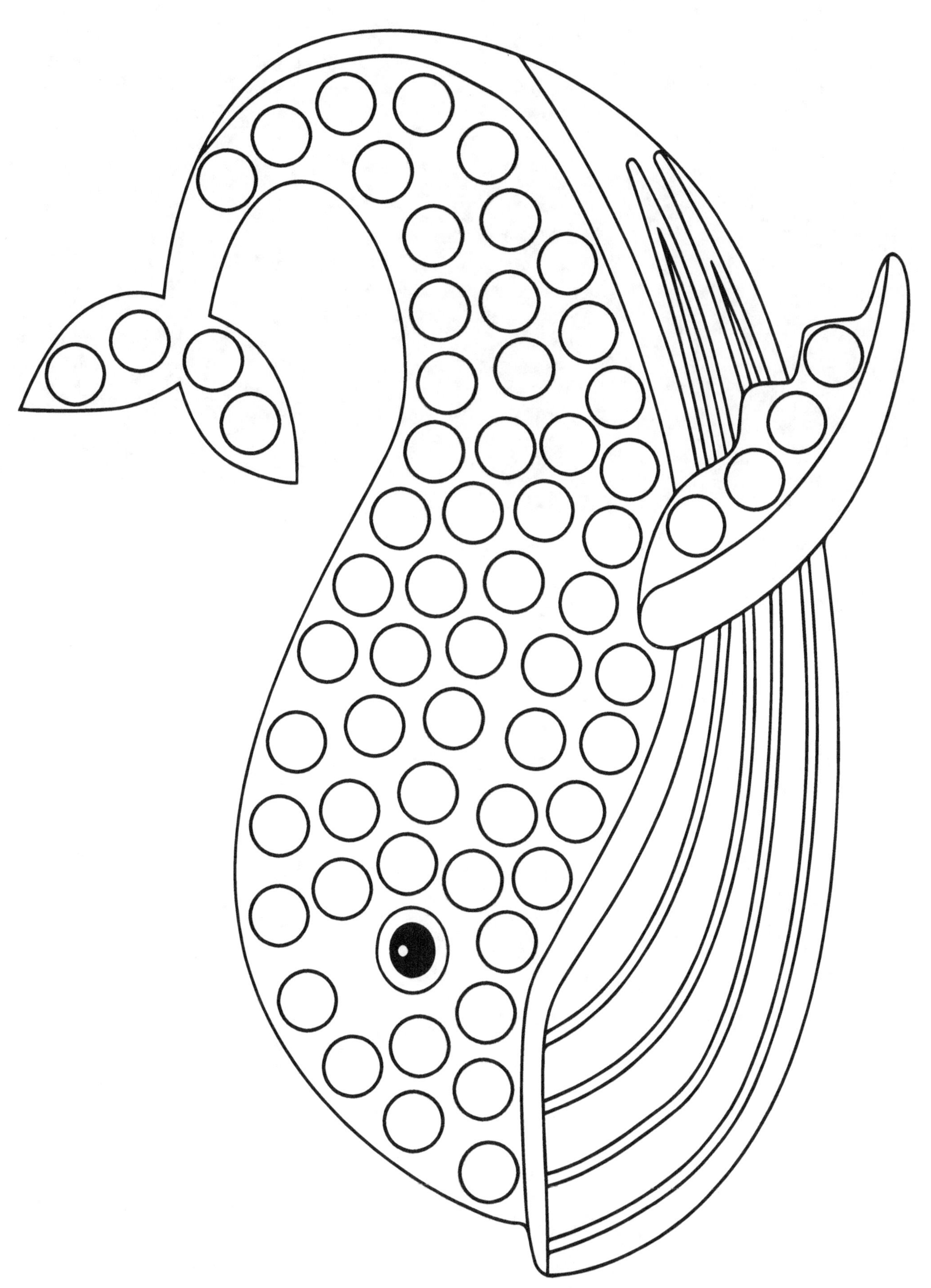

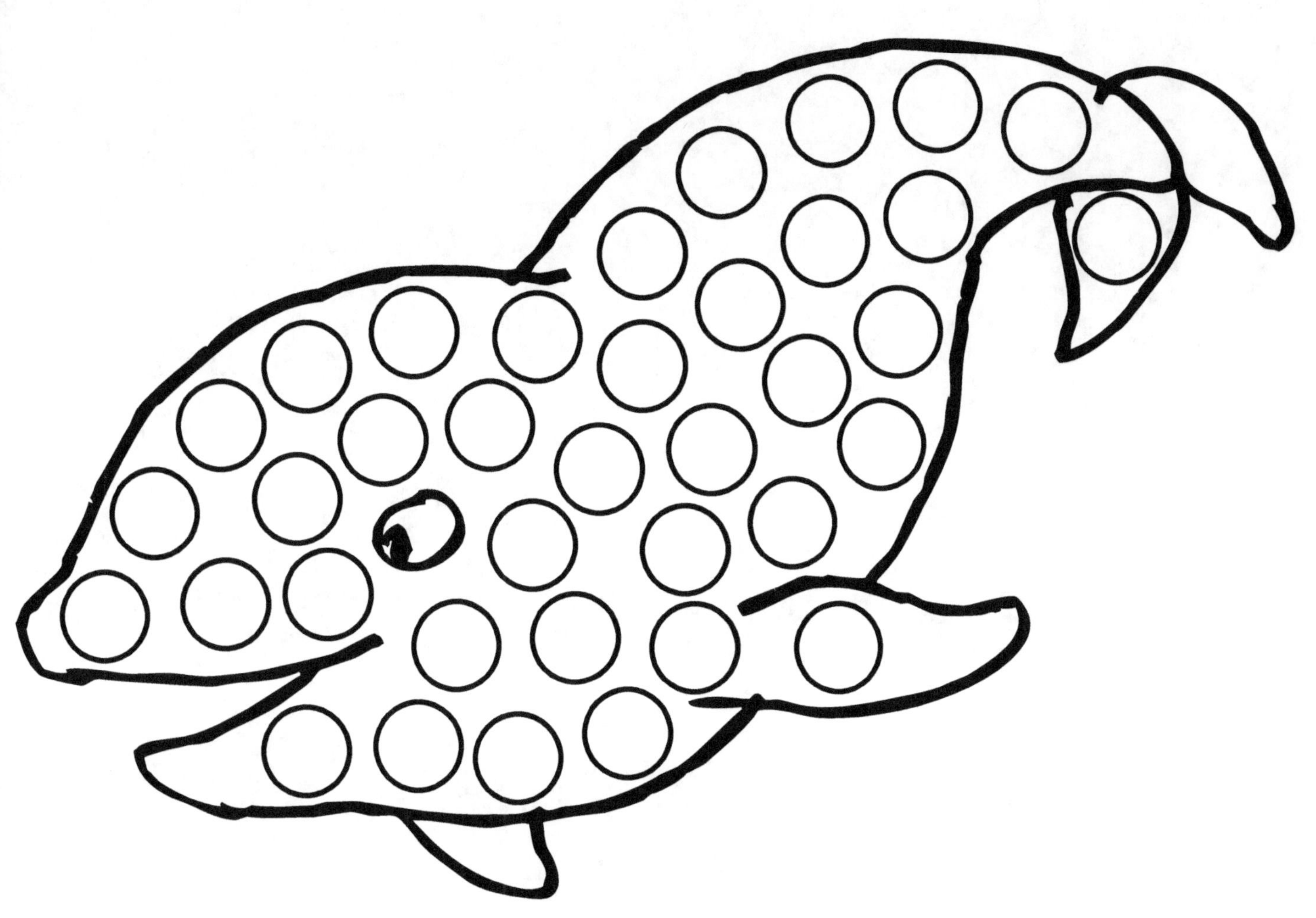

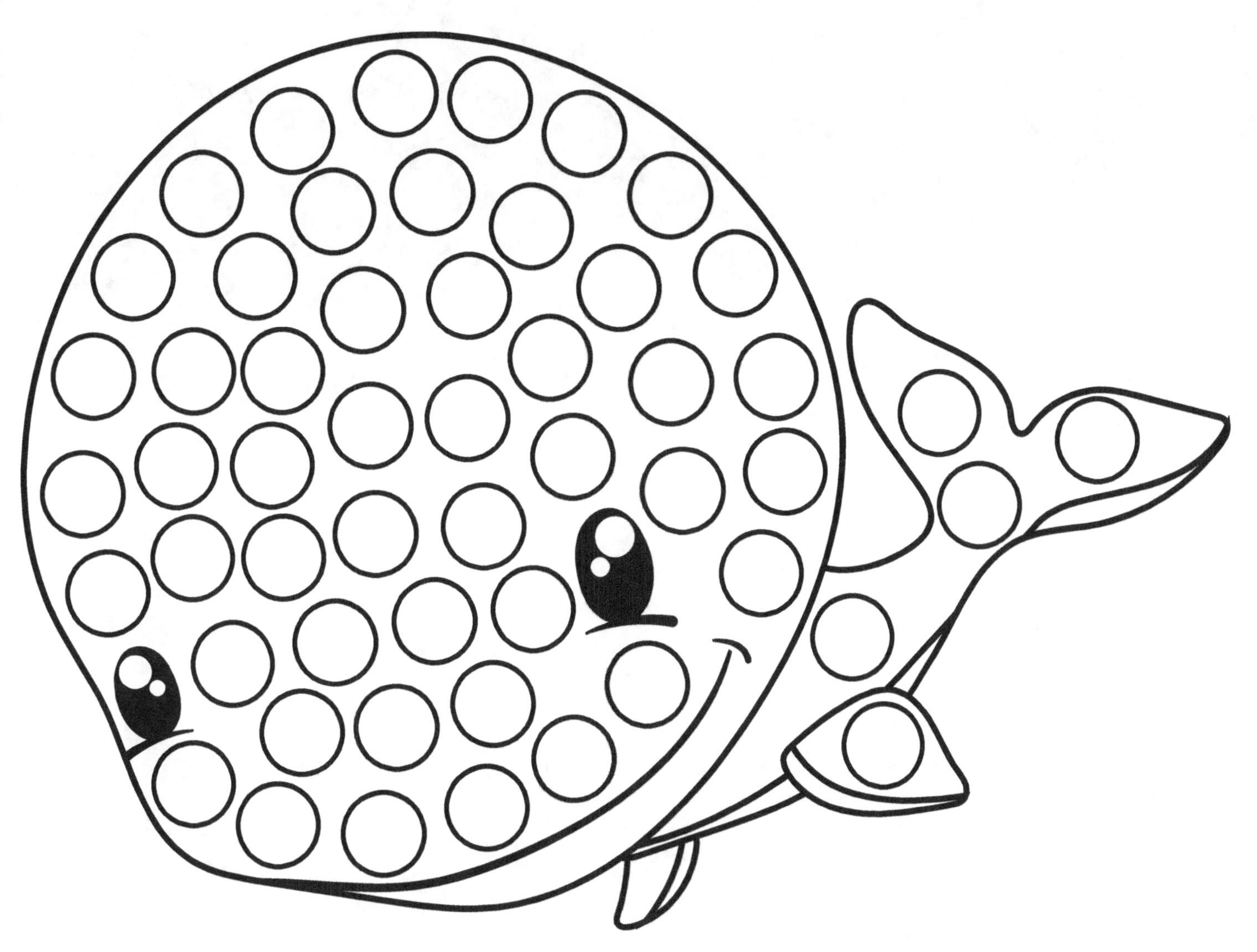

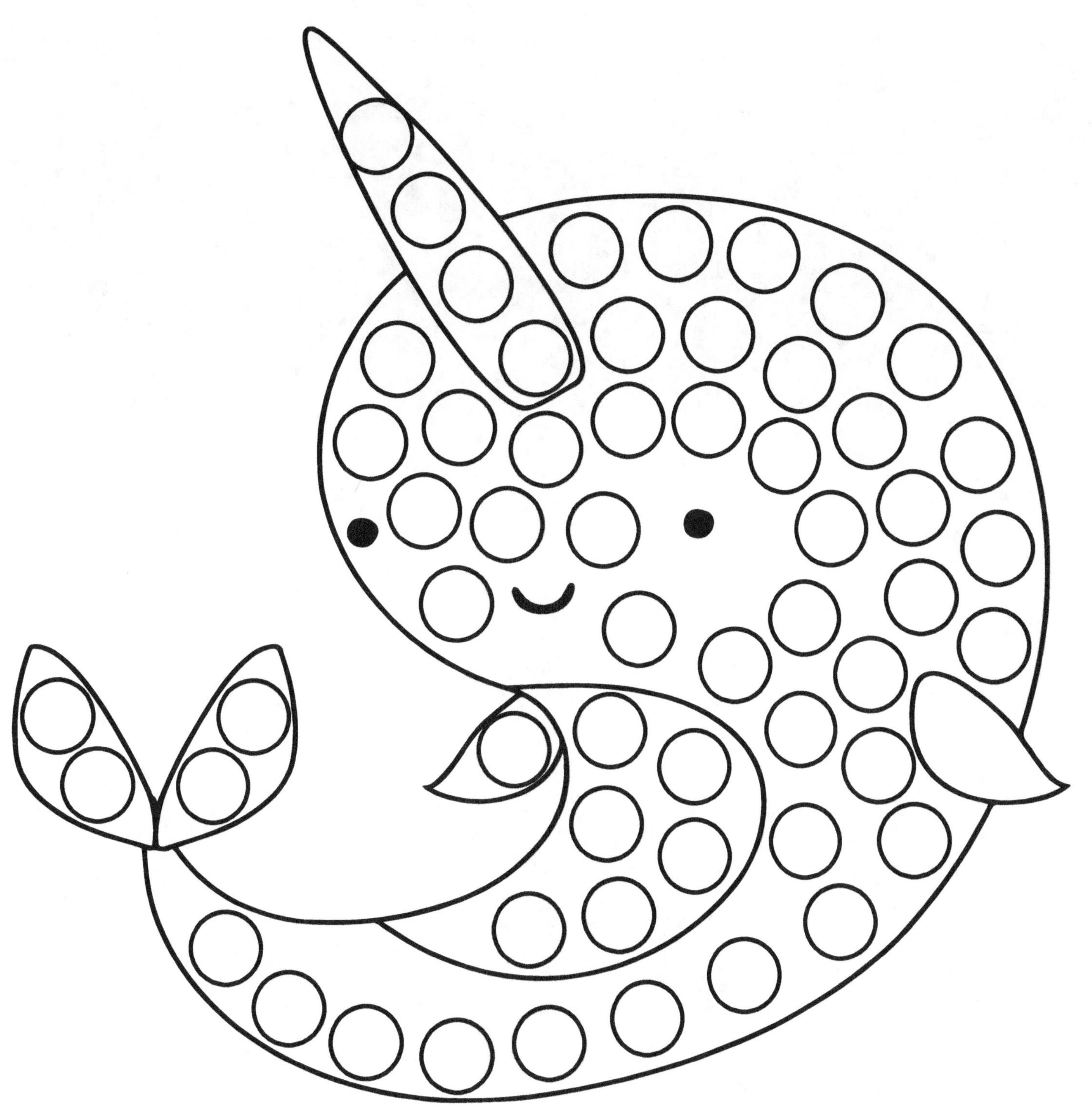

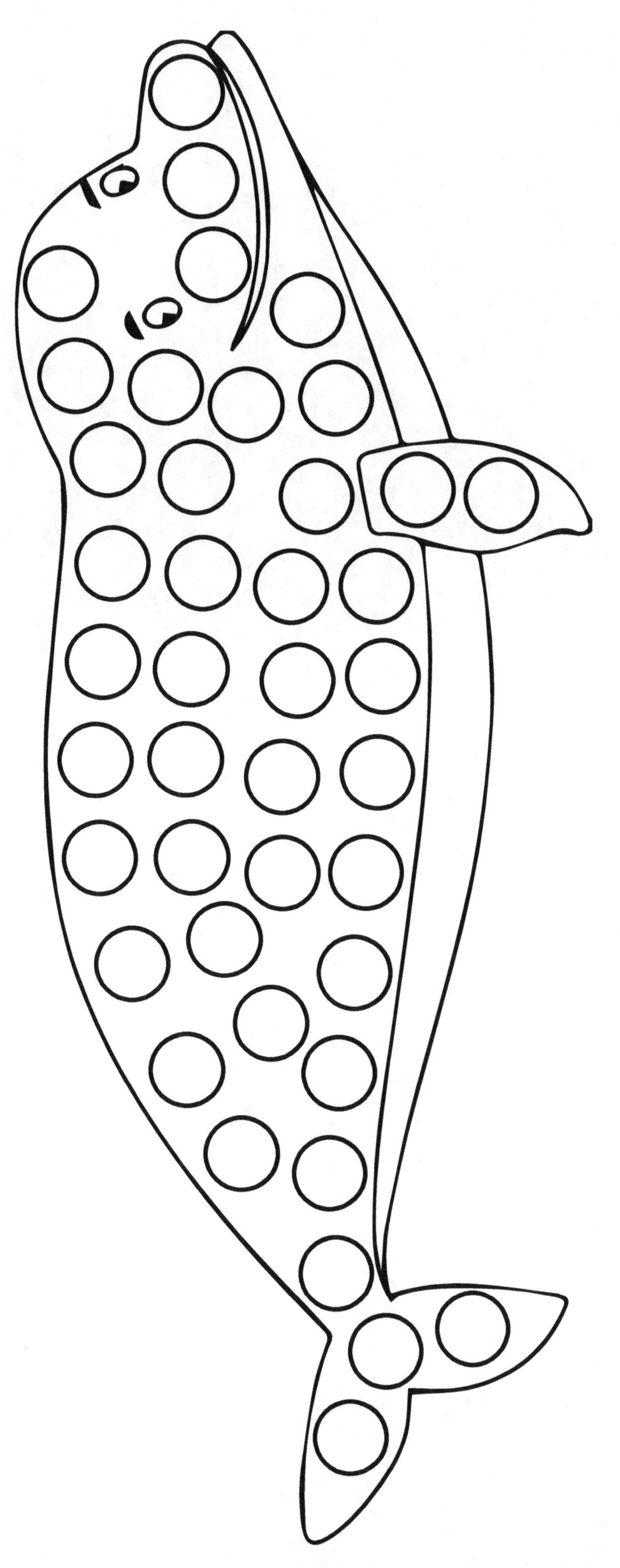

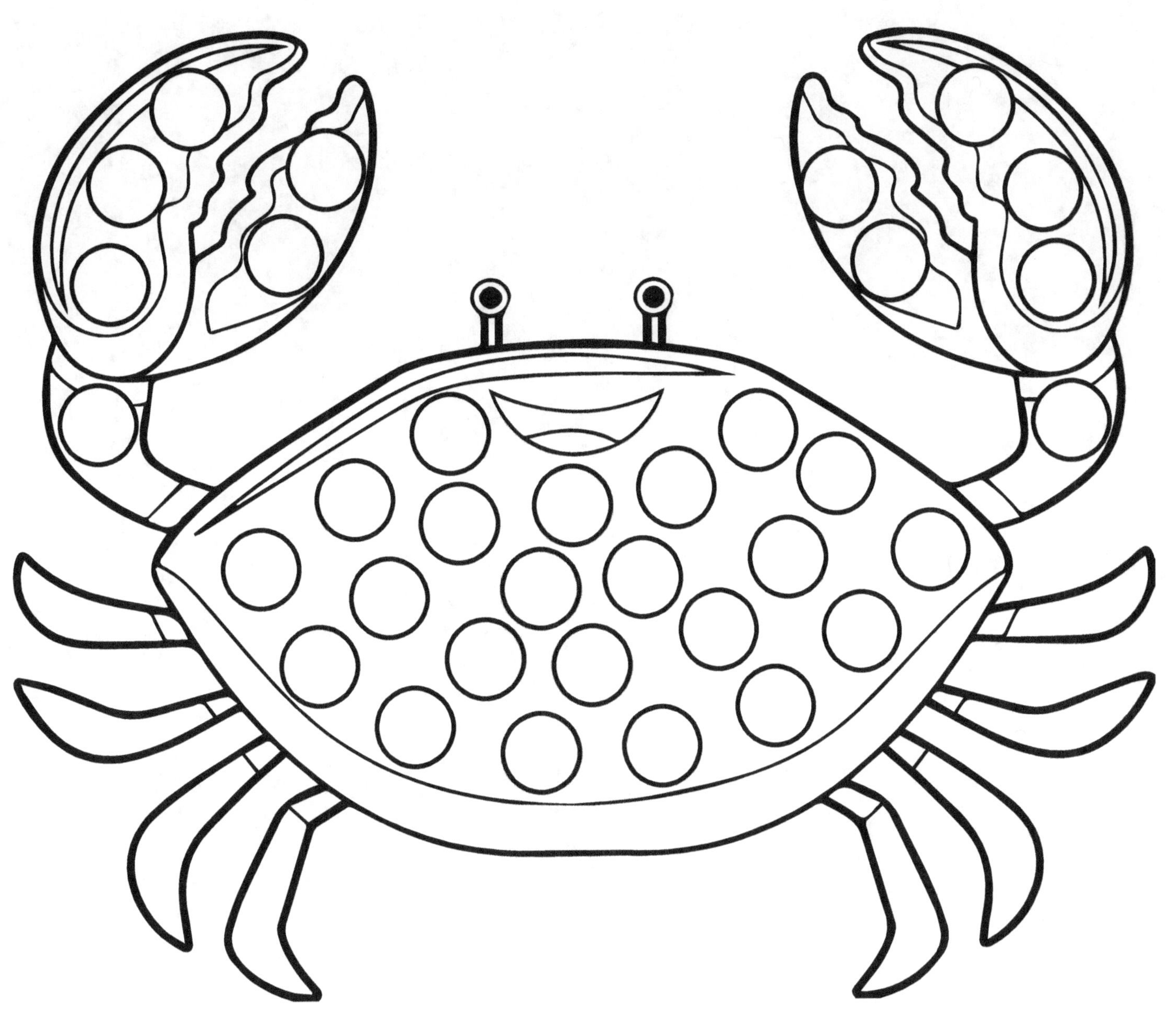

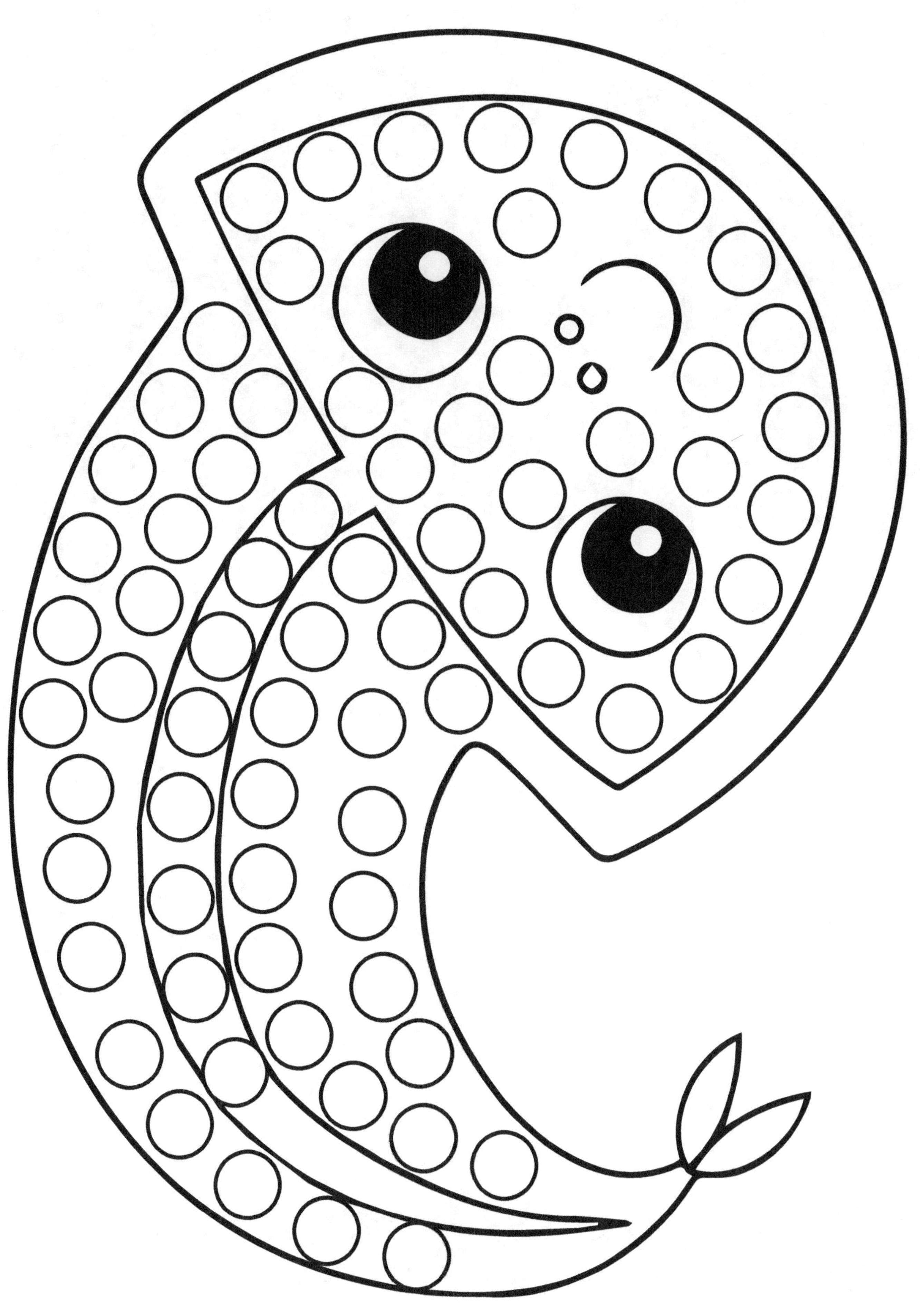

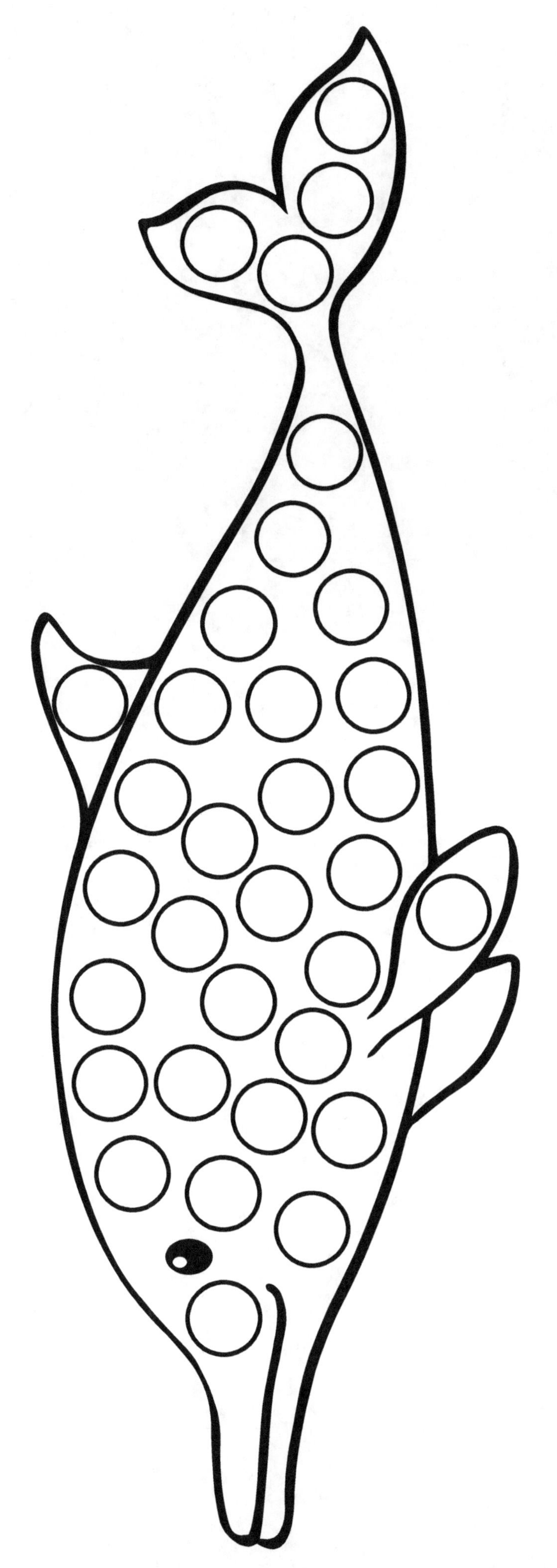

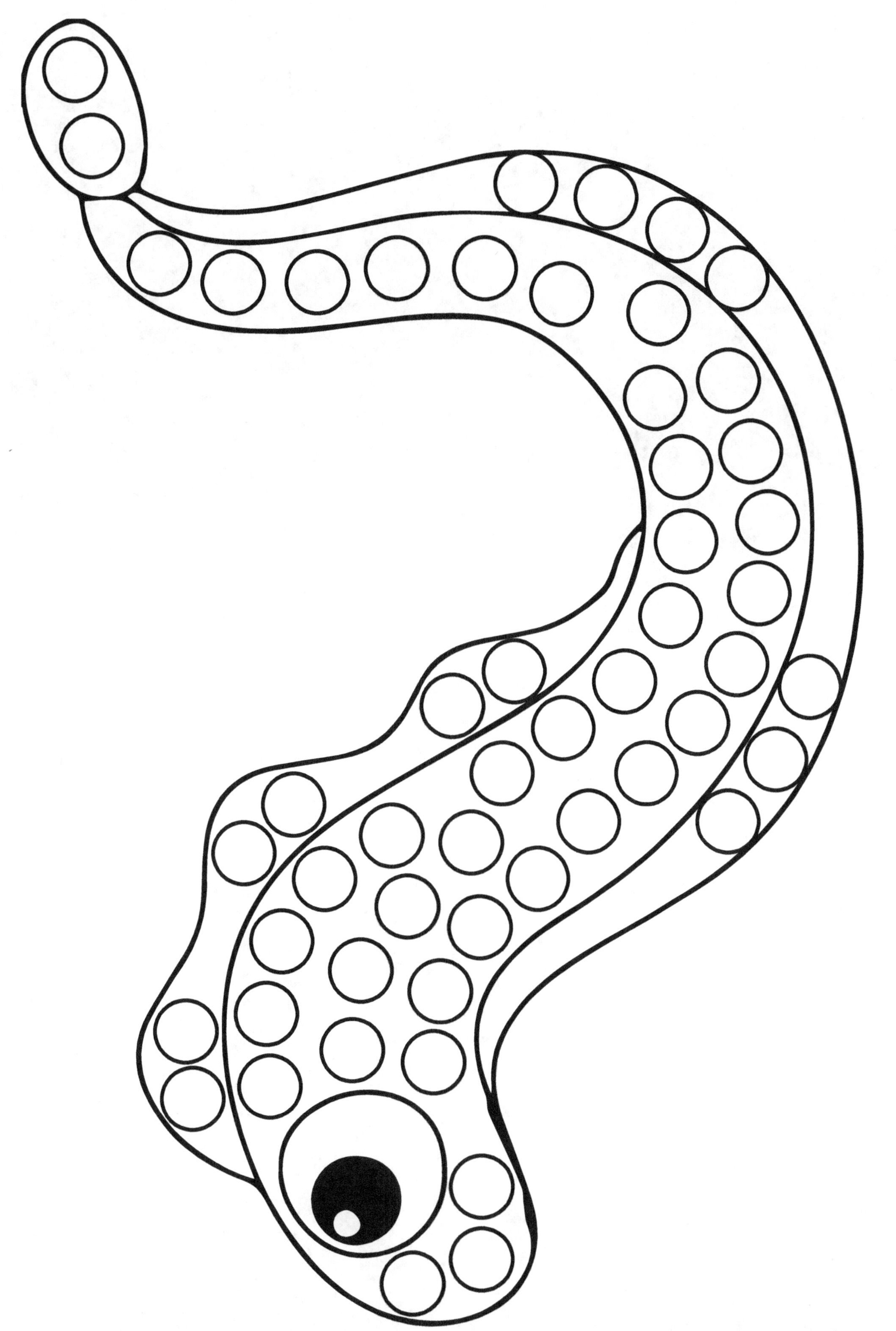

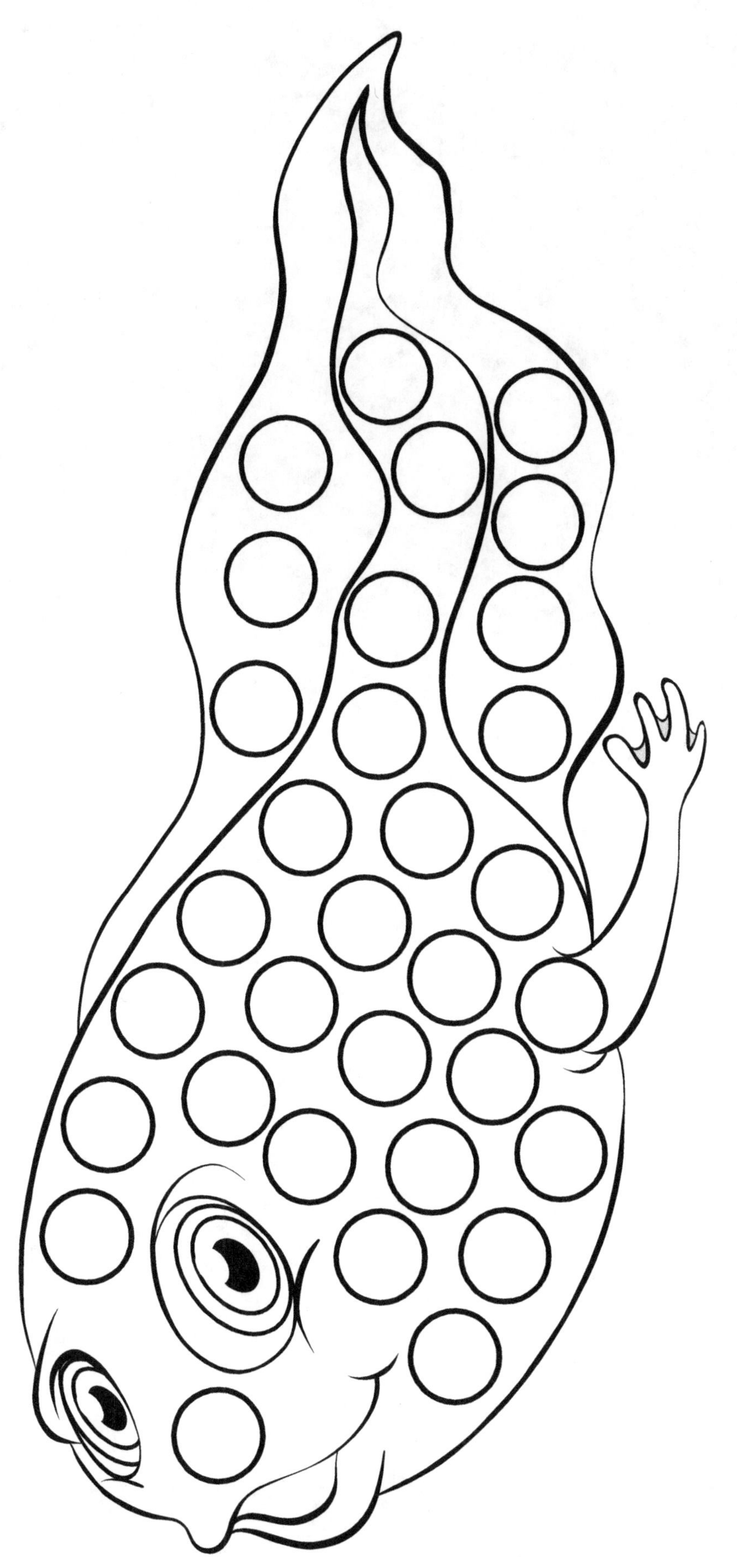

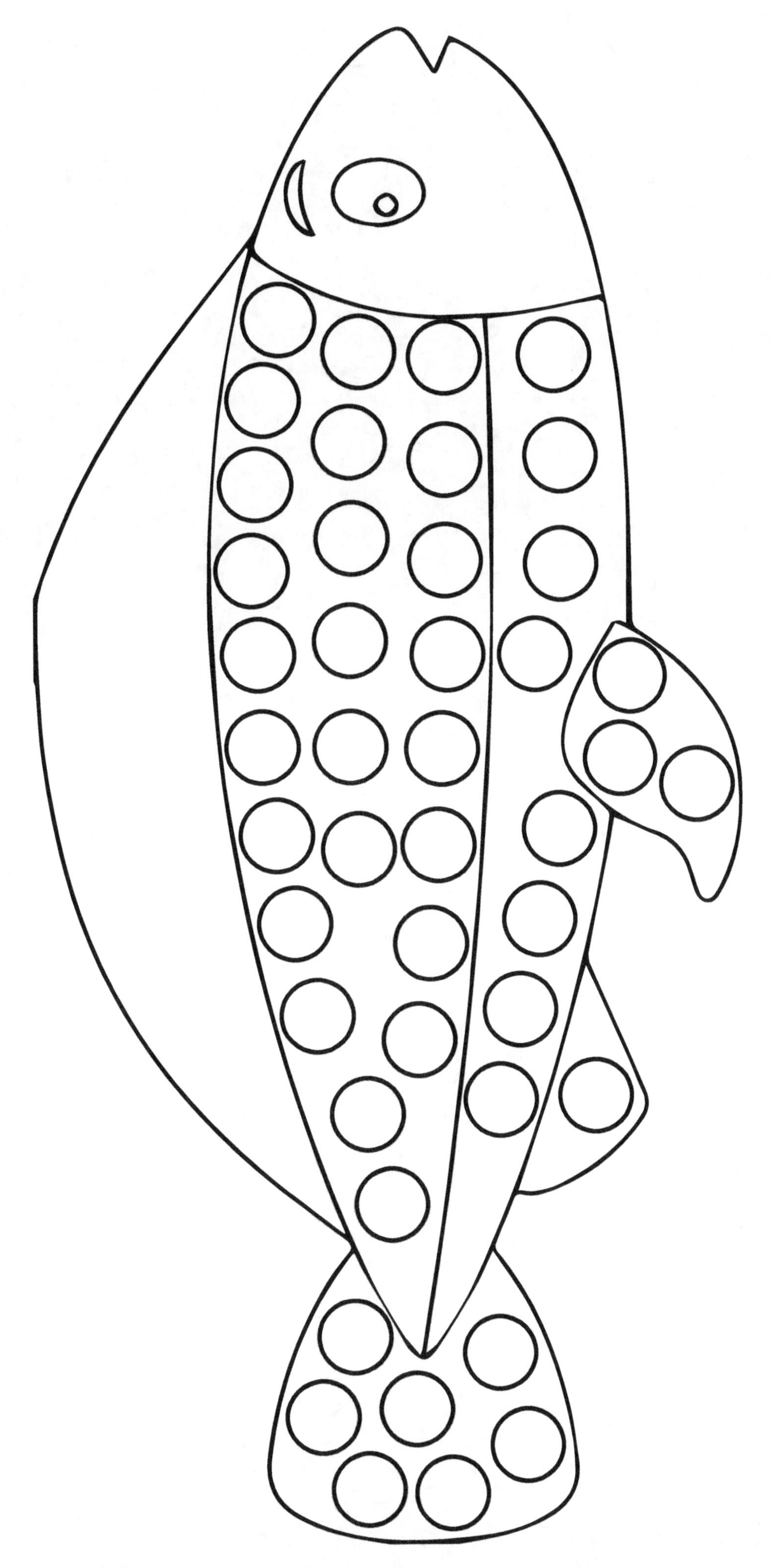

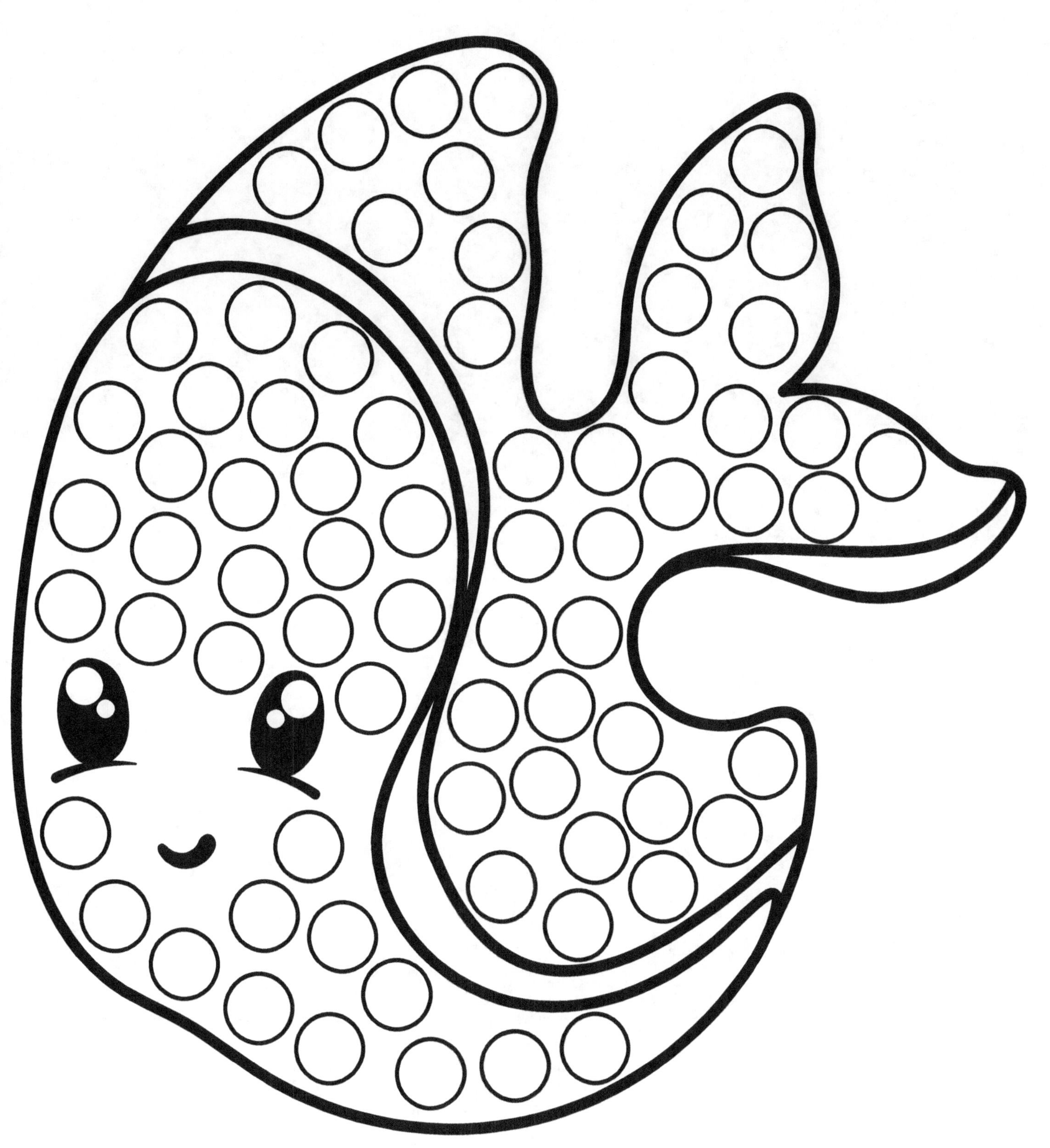